Liberated Publishing

Presents:

TRY
ME

An Essential Collection of Poems
Presented By:

Andrus D. Love, MS

LiberatedPublishing.com

Liberated Publishing Inc.
1860 Wilma Rudolph Blvd
Clarksville, TN 37040

Published by: Liberated Publishing Inc

ISBN: 978-0-9895732-7-6

First Printing: April 2015

I look forward to establishing trust
within each individual
concerning future projects. These
pages will appeal to people
who appreciate artistic expression
in the form of poetry.
May my words
as well as life experiences
bless you and I both.

Andrus Demond Love, MS

B.S. Criminal Justice/ Sociology   UAB
M.S. Clinical Psychology/ Counseling   Troy
University

Table of Contents

Encouragement/ Growth

Love

Religion

5/23/07

Times are hard, everyday it gets sad
One may ask, how would you
make it Without being blessed
with a mom and dad

Killing on a daily basis, smoking blunts
With laces, not understanding
Responsibilities But still making babies,
got us asking what's wrong

Hold on my people hold on would
Be a statement of encouragement
But you got soldiers dying everyday
Some due to insurgents

With the daily hassle of gas prices
Spiraling out of control Racism, Hatred, and
Violence, We must all act, Unite, Take
A Stand and say NO

Questions

Questions often gives us answers,
things we tend not to believe.
The world is full of questions that
one man has yet to achieve.
Questions raised in the moment of matter
gives us a stance to recognize.
Trusting yourself is merely words,
Applying is more worthy
of challenging by disguise.
Questions teaches one to learn,
while throwing caution to discern.
Questions allows us to grow,
whether maturation comes fast or slow.
Questions do not consider,
they show!

Colors

Colors can be made in your mind
With disregards to one specific sight
Light is night, but one must rewind

Colors can be rich and or smooth
Mixed, matched, rearranged to be
come one Close your eyes and choose

Colors can be uplifting and destroying
too Colors can range from one to a few
Colors can be lovely or loveless

Which one are you

Rally

Renting Resting Roaring Receiving

Accepting Accomplishing Acquiring
Achieving

Loving Learning Lending Leaping

Lighting Laughing Lifting Leaving

Yearning Yielding Yanking Yelling

I AM

I am, I am that somebody who fits all descriptions.
I am, I am that person who is the subject, not
subjected to crime.
I am, I am the one who did it.
I am, I am the one who got blamed.
I am, I am the seller, buyer and the supplier.
I am, I am not simple nor complex.
I am, I am one of the many.
I am, I am riding on the dream.
I am, I am colored like a penny.
I am, I am a commodity, the cream.
I am, I am educated taking a stand.
I am, I am a Black Man.

Sexy You

Sipping on a glass of you Would be elegant sweetness
Your heart paired with raw beauty
Calls out stubborn developing meekness
Sexy you
Fixed with the right frame sporting classic
Styles and pedicure toes is her game
Got me posting up physically Tagging you with my last
name
Sexy you
Love signs achieve new levels Associating themselves
with you
Like softness echoing off your fingertips
Riding the clouds amongst the blues
Sexy you
Watching your graceful steps Away and towards me
Immediately ignites a flame within
That will burn eternally
Sexy you
Competition can not compete cause The beat that you
walk to when
you hit the street is not click
clack or Pity pat it is unique
Sexy You
When I see you pictured in my mind I am right there by
your side
Complimenting your masterpiece here
Is your sexiness baby to this we ride
Sexy You

11

Anniversary

*A*nticipation from seeing a

*N*ew face is what I felt

*N*ewly weds we soon became when

I do was declared

*V*ows we took

*E*veryday we cherish

*R*ealizing the love we

*S*hare is

*A*lways and forever

*R*eadily I say I Love

*Y*ou

14

Ten Years

Ten years is like one loving you
Because it is all still new
Girl life itself is blessed
forgive me for the caused moments- Stressed

Ten years, boy how times fly
Fly is how I feel, Stupid when
You my wife, continues to be Real
Sometimes I need to pass on by

Ten years is the last time I said I do
Proposing my life forever
Help me girl, I want to be True
Loving me with no hesitation, how clever

Ten years you have showed me a new me
Keeping the faith, never wavering and waiting steadily
Holding you tightly, often and intensely is my key
Devoting ten more years plus to loving you,
Passionately

11/03/09

The mere thought of you pleases me
Down to the depths of my soul
Mind tingling and body snatching
Moments are what I long for
Until the day I grow old

Loving you is like loving me
The price paid for your essence are
Examples of experiences most people will not
see

Living for the hour, minute or even second
Your heart was captured by my surprise
Leaves me yearning for the time your
Sweet voice echoes my name and
To the call I answer, I rise

Love Levels

Top heavy, swaying when the wind blows as she
walks down the street. Picking up the stride
smiling and watching while systematically
walking to the beat. Warm sensations
created to please allows me to unwind
and plug up to experience the heat.
Sheltered and scattered abroad dispensing
love tokens near and far.
Moving viciously looking to settle, intensely
shifting moods like one hitting switches
on a car. Follow me, follow me a
sweet voice whispers and as time flows
the soul weeps. Longing for a gentle clue,
the inner circle dissolves as the new
design peeps. Reaching, pulling and
tugging at this thing called love.
Devouring the essence of the mood
which flies freely like a newly released dove.
Triggering the thought of being obsessed.
Caressing the mind while teasing the body to rest.
Painting a picture that captures the last cry
her times ten is my daily medication until I die.

Back To School

Because God lives I am able to fall
And get back up in order to realize I
Can call upon his name and together we can
Kick the bad and focus on the good

Today is a new day, yesterday never returns. So
Open your eyes and say I am ready to learn

Should I or can I display my abilities and enhance or
Create new qualities that I will appreciate within this
House, that serves as initial preparation for the
future
Or will I fall victim to temptation and get kicked
Out and ruin all chances to have a career because of
Lazy no good habits

Back To School

Used to ... and live-I am able to tell
and get he die that (rate to realize ...
Can call up ... his name and to call have car
th ... the bad and look up too good ...

Today is a new day, a brand new routine. So
Open your eyes and say I am ready to learn

Now ... I can ... I display my ability ... and enhance on
Create new abilities that I will appreciate within his
People that ... as initial preparation for life

... I fall ... felt up to temptation and get kicked
O and ... all things I have ... and ... because ...
Easy people, know ...

22

Untitled

Not all who begin reaches the end
With blocks and trenches along the way
Most people who strive to be good, Sin

Heavy, beaten and sometimes bruised
Always yearning and eager to climb
Dirty people become clean after being misused

Reach for the unattainable treasures within the earth
Please be assured and rest to achieve
Life was granted a second chance in relation to the birth

09/14/09

To love or not to Love is the question
One must be lost in order to be found
Expect, exceed, explore and stop bugging
Ask yourself is it Love or am I just lusting

The things you want in life may not be free
Correct the wrongs, and simply let it be
Truly live today by example for tomorrow
Tears full of joy sometimes override sorrow

Let your life serve as a Beacon to most
Are you the fuel that flame the fire
The bird in one hand or Casper the friendly ghost
Relax, relate, and release the urge within named Desire

Fail and fail again because that symbolizes a genuine try
Be careful because living only begins when you die
Success is measured in minutes with a humble fly
A man is not a man if he will not cry

Problems

Problems, problems are universal and chaotic in nature
They create, display and even provoke anger
Inside, outside, around and about The date people have
with problems Is persistent and calls you out
Problems have no friends
They attempt to make amends with
the devil but how deep Is your hole, because in the
hands
of the enemy is the shovel
They affect every color regardless of the mindset
Test after test you will fail until you get it
Why me one constantly pleads The life he gave was to
save
yours Until the very end he continues to bleed
Why is a question that is asked but rarely seen
growth is personal but what does this mean
Living life can deliver a hard blow, so bend your knees,
Open your heart and hang your head low
Trust and Believe, divine intervention; ultimately you
will receive

Revelation

One may add that everything seems to be easy
but in actuality it is hard. Hard to the fact that
every task is able to be dissected. Taking apart
at the very seam, the twinkle in your eye is really
a beam. Beaming with the radiant vibe of every
Heart beat that stops at the time of expiration.
Expired but not Deceased is the obstacle we are
all faced with. Many blocks are Built to create
a stumbling effect within the world. The world
is as cold as it is hot. Therefore, understanding
the distinct degrees of the mind will allow one to
have favor. Favor to deal with the negative in
a positive mood. The movement which eliminates
the desire to give in, give up, or get out. Out is
Really inside the boundaries that have been
formulated from within. Within is a pleasure
principle that is stimulated due to fear. Fear of
having the unknown revealed to the thought
of your faith being tested

Revelation

I appreciate your thoughtfulness and needed Consideration. For those kind acts of sincerity to allow part of my life to be in yours, I hope something in the previous pages Truly blessed or positively motivated you in some way.
Thank You in advance for sharing, recommending and socializing. You have invested personally towards the Legacy of another Alabama Poet/Author.

Andrus D. Love is an educated mentor, visionary, trainer, author, poet as well as a compassionate leader. He has a lovely wife and four beautiful children. Andrus believes all people are important with unique qualities and distinctive characteristics. He strives to be an optimist in the midst of problematic times mixed with sorrowful situations; while enhancing individuals' knowledge of how to manage everyday life. The University of Alabama at Birmingham (U.A.B.) allowed him to gain a Bachelor's Degree in Criminal Justice/Sociology; which he completed in 2001. He also graduated from Troy University with honors in Clinical Psychology & Counseling to obtain a Master's Degree in 2011. Overall, Andrus uses his personal experiences to give others a different perspective in life that permits them to adapt and or overcome!

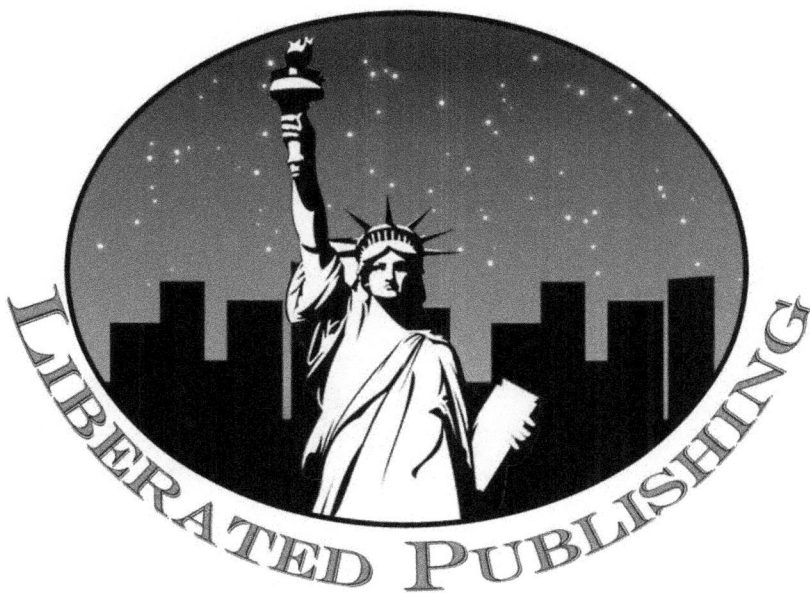

Liberated Publishing Inc.
1860 Wilma Rudolph Blvd
Clarksville, TN 37040
info@liberatedpublishing.com
931-378-0500

www.LiberatedPublishing.com